THIS BOOK
BELONGS TO

_____

MAD

BY THER

Ariel Books · Andrews

ONNA

SA CELSI

l McMeel · Kansas City

Cover photo: Mike Guastella / Star File

All photographs courtesy of the Star File Photo Agency and their photographers: Max Goldstein, Chuck Pulin, Bob Grune, Vinnie Zuffante, Bob Leafe, Gene Shaw, Danny Chin.

ISBN: 0-8362-3043-4

Library of Congress Catalog Card Number: 93-70470

"I SOMETIMES THINK I WAS BORN TO LIVE UP TO MY NAME. HOW COULD I BE ANYTHING ELSE BUT WHAT I AM, HAVING BEEN NAMED MADONNA? I WOULD EITHER HAVE ENDED UP A NUN OR THIS."

A STAR IS BORN

She was born Madonna Louise Veronica Ciccone. Now, thirtysomething years later, she is known simply as Madonna. One name — like Caesar, Napoleon, Michelangelo. But legends are not made overnight, and the journey from Madonna Louise Veronica Ciccone to Madonna began on August 16, 1958.

Madonna was the third child of Silvio (known as Tony) and Madonna Ciccone, middle-class Catholics living in Pontiac, Michigan. When she was six, her mother died of cancer. This shattering loss led her to feel an almost obsessive need for control and attention.

Always headstrong, young Madonna

exploded into fiery rebellion a few years later when her father remarried. She was hell-bent on breaking whatever rules she could. For example, she rebelled against the standard

madonna ciccone

Catholic school uniform by wearing brightly colored underwear; and to make sure everyone knew, she hung upside-down on the monkey bars at recess.

STRAIGHT-A REBEL

Despite her behavior, Madonna was a straight-A student, partly because of her intelligence (her IQ is over 140) but mostly due to her father. An engineer, Tony Ciccone was the first in his family to graduate from college, and he demanded academic excellence from his children. As Madonna puts it, "If my father hadn't been strict, I wouldn't be who I am today. I think that his strictness taught me a certain amount of discipline that has helped me in my life and my career and also made me work harder for things, whether for acceptance or the privilege to do things."

In high school, that hard work won

Madonna a 4.0 average, two years on the cheerleading squad, and starring roles in school productions.   She also did volunteer work for Help A Kid.

It was a busy schedule, but not busy enough to keep Madonna out of trouble.   She hung out with the local bikers and got into cat fights with their girlfriends.   Even though her father ordered her to attend mass, she usually found ways to skip services; she and her girlfriends would show up wearing overcoats with nothing on underneath, giggling at the idea of being in church naked.   They also peeked through their teachers' windows at night, curious to see what the nuns wore under their habits. What Madonna Louise needed was a direction for her tremendous energy. She found it in a ballet class.

A MENTOR

Having taken jazz dance classes for years, Madonna decided to switch to ballet, so her parents enrolled her at a local dance studio. Fourteen-year-old Madonna entered the classes at a disadvantage since the other girls her age had been studying ballet's exacting technique for years. But she worked hard to catch up, and that determination impressed her teacher, Christopher Flynn.

One day during a break, while Madonna

was sitting with her hair wrapped in a towel, Flynn took a good look at her face. "You're really beautiful," he told her. "You have an ancient-looking face. A face like an ancient Roman statue." She had been called many things, but no one had ever called her beautiful.

Madonna's beauty was not the only quality Flynn saw. He understood her spirit, her desire for artistic expression, and her longing for sexual freedom. Madonna adored Flynn, calling him "my mentor, my father, my imaginative lover, my brother, everything because he understood me."

Flynn woke Madonna up. He took her to museums and galleries, taught her about art and music, and helped her win a dance scholarship to the University of Michigan's School of Music. However, she wasn't at U of M long before she was ready for even bigger things.

"I HAVE THE SAME GOAL I'VE
HAD SINCE I WAS A LITTLE
GIRL: I WANT TO RULE THE
WORLD!"

"TO ME, THE WHOLE PROCESS
OF BEING A BRUSHSTROKE IN
SOMEONE ELSE'S PAINTING IS
A LITTLE DIFFICULT. I'M
USED TO BEING IN CHARGE
OF EVERYTHING."

NEXT STOP: THE BIG APPLE

On Flynn's advice, Madonna decided to go to New York. She saved enough money for a one-way ticket, and in the middle of August 1976, carrying a single bag and her teddy bear and wearing her winter coat, Madonna landed in the Big Apple.

She told the cab driver to take her to the "center of everything," so, of course, he dropped her off in Times Square. After paying the fare, she had all of twenty-two dollars, no place to live, and no friends to turn to. A good Samaritan let her stay with him until she could find a job and a place to live.

Her first apartment was in a tenement

on Fourth Street in New York's East Village. The hallways were infested with roaches and rats; the streets were infested with junkies and dealers.

Madonna actively pursued her dancing career. She was accepted by the Alvin Ailey and Pearl Lang dance company schools. At Ailey, she took classes with the third-string dancers, but with Lang she scored a solo role in *I Never Saw a Butterfly*.

To pay her rent, she took menial jobs at Dunkin' Donuts, Burger King, and the famous Russian Tea Room. But her meager earnings often weren't enough for food or rent. More than once, she scrounged meals from garbage cans, and she learned to live with what she could carry so that she could crash on friends' couches and floors.

She made a bit of money by posing nude for art and photography classes. Unlike some models, Madonna was not shy about getting naked. "You have to remove yourself from everyone looking at you," she later said. "It's a job. But I knew that those people were not just looking at me aesthetically."

Madonna began seeing a man named Dan Gilroy. One day, Gilroy showed her how to play a few chords on the guitar, and something clicked. She latched onto the idea of music as a career. She and Gilroy put together a band,

"I'M TOUGH, AMBITIOUS, AND I KNOW EXACTLY WHAT I WANT. IF THAT MAKES ME A BITCH, OKAY."

"MY MOVIE COMPANY IS SIREN FILMS. YOU KNOW WHAT A SIREN IS, DON'T YOU? A WOMAN WHO LEADS MEN TO THEIR DEATHS."

and Madonna started writing songs. But the band's career was interrupted by the kind of thing that happens only in movies . . . or in the life of Madonna.

To Paris and Back

In 1979, Madonna answered an ad in *Variety* magazine to dance and sing backup for a French singer. The producers were so impressed with the way Madonna belted out her audition song that they hired her — not to sing backup but to make her a star. Suddenly, Madonna was on her way to money and fame — and Paris.

Paris was a huge disappointment. Although the producers gave Madonna singing and dancing coaches, they were more interested in showing her off as a New York punk curiosity than in actually creating material for her. Pleading homesickness, she told them she wanted to visit her family. Back in New York, she rejoined Dan Gilroy's band briefly, then decided to form her own.

The drummer in the new band was Steve Bray, whom Madonna had dated when they were both students at the University of Michigan. Madonna and Bray moved in together and began playing in Lower East Side dives. After about a year the band fell apart, but by this time Madonna had the confidence to strike out on her own.

Using a combination of brattiness and ballsiness, she enticed manager Camille Barbone to come to a gig. Barbone immediately signed her up, got her an apartment and a housekeeping job, and began putting together a band.

Barbone pushed Madonna to make her sound light. For two years, Madonna pretended to follow her advice, but at night she and Bray perfected the harder sound she preferred. Just when the agent was on the verge of getting Madonna a record deal, Madonna left her. Once again, Madonna walked away from success on somebody else's terms.

A DEAL OF ONE'S OWN

Madonna and Bray recorded a new demo tape
that she persuaded Mark Kamins, the deejay at
New York's famous Danceteria, to play. The
crowd went wild. Kamins played the tape
for the executives at Sire Records, who were
as impressed with Madonna as they were with
her sound. She and Bray were signed to record
a single.

Or so they thought. Kamins had been
invaluable in setting up the deal and insisted
on producing the record. Madonna, who had
already promised Bray he could produce, was
forced to choose between Bray and the deal.
She chose the deal. It wasn't the first time —

or the last — Madonna would betray someone who had helped her.

The finished single was called "Ain't No Big Deal," with a B side called "Everybody." After deciding the recording of "Ain't No Big

"ALL THOSE MEN I STEPPED ALL OVER TO GET TO THE TOP — EVERY ONE OF THEM WOULD TAKE ME BACK BECAUSE THEY STILL LOVE ME AND I STILL LOVE THEM."

"YOU CAN BE A BITCH UNTIL YOUR HEART'S BROKEN, AND WHEN YOUR HEART'S BROKEN, YOU'RE A SUPERBITCH ABOUT EVERYTHING EXCEPT THAT."

Deal" was terrible, a Sire executive made an unorthodox decision to release "Everybody" on both sides. It was a brilliant move. The record climbed steadily up the dance charts to become a hit. The video pushed it onto the Pop 100 chart as well. Then Sire put out a twelve-inch version.

By now Madonna was able to insist that Kamins be replaced, dumping him as she had dumped Bray. It was the right decision, though; Kamins couldn't produce the sound she wanted. Her new producer, Reggie Lucas, wrote "Physical Attraction" for her. When it became her second hit, Sire gave Madonna the green light for an album.

Her first album, *Madonna*, produced six
Top Ten dance hits. It was not just her songs
that sold the album, it was Madonna. Her out-
rageous sense of style inspired a national craze
among teens and shocked their parents. Her
rosaries-as-jewelry, her lacy underwear worn
on the outside of her clothes, her Boy Toy belt
buckle, and her tousled hairstyle became part
of an instantly recognizable persona.

Madonna's second album, *Like a Virgin*,
clinched her success and launched a nationwide tour. After years of walking away from
people who tried to mold her, she had finally
found the perfect image — her own.

LOVE AND MOVIES

It was on the set of her "Material Girl" video
that Madonna first saw her future husband,
Sean Penn — a brooding leather-clad presence
standing off in a corner. Their meeting was
oddly fitting: Penn, a disciple of method acting,
was reminiscent of fifties actor James Dean,
while Madonna was consciously re-creating for
the video another fifties star, Marilyn Monroe.
They were two iconic wannabes, reborn into a
new generation.

Soon, Penn and Madonna were secretly
dating. However, the headlines were full of a
romance between her and rock star Prince.
The Prince connection was mainly a publicity

ploy, but it incited Penn's jealousy. One night, angered by the press coverage, he put his fist through Madonna's wall. He beat up photographers who followed the couple and even pummeled one of her friends, whom he mistook for a lover.

These actions should have been a warning to Madonna; instead, they excited her. Although Penn was raised in the opulence of Beverly Hills, he actively cultivated a street-tough image. Madonna, who had actually lived a tough street life, was attracted to his dangerous aura.

While she was dating Penn, her third movie, *Desperately Seeking Susan*, was released.

The part of Susan was written for Diane Keaton. When she didn't work out, director Susan Seidelman decided Madonna would be perfect for the role. But the studio needed convincing. Madonna was unknown as an actress. Her only other acting roles had been a waitress in *A Certain Sacrifice* and a rock singer in *Vision Quest*, in which she performed two of her songs.

As it turned out, Madonna was so close to the character that she didn't need to act. And she impressed everyone with her professionalism. While many people needed a wake-up call to get to the set on time, Madonna arrived promptly every morning after working out at her health club.

"As much as people complain and criticize me, I've touched a nerve in them somehow."

"I still believe in God.... I believe in everything. That's what Catholicism teaches you."

"I'm not interested in doing things I'm not in."

Madonna also contributed a song to the film, "Into the Groove," which she and Steve Bray had written. A video of Madonna dancing to the song, intercut with clips of the film, was released to MTV. It was an instant hit, and the song became the top radio request — before it was even released. This publicity certainly helped the film, but so did Madonna's performance. She was funny and attractive, the critics were approving, and people flocked to the movie, making it one of the year's top grossers.

SCANDALS AND MARRIAGE

The same year *Desperately Seeking Susan* was released, Madonna launched her nationwide

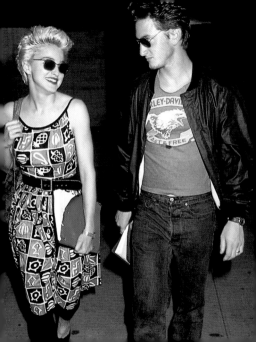

Virgin Tour. Sean Penn attended the concerts in Miami, Santa Barbara, and Detroit. After the Detroit show, Madonna introduced him to her parents. She met his when the tour hit Los Angeles. In June, they became engaged. And in July, scandal hit.

Penthouse magazine had discovered some photographs taken of Madonna in 1979, when she had been a nude model. A year before, they had published a similar "exposé" of Miss America, Vanessa Williams. Shortly after *Penthouse*'s announcement, *Playboy* magazine declared that it, too, had nude pictures of Madonna. *Penthouse*'s edition hit the newsstands first, on July 10, 1985.

Other women had been devastated by such scandals: Vanessa Williams had been forced to give up her crown; Marilyn Monroe had pleaded for sympathy from her adoring fans. But Madonna was more concerned that she had no control over the pictures. She couldn't stop the publication, nor would she get a cent from them. Unlike Williams and Monroe, she was unabashed by the controversy. She hadn't been ashamed of the pictures then and saw no reason to be ashamed now.

Not so with Penn. He flipped out when even her gay friends kissed her on the cheek. Now every man in the country could have nude pictures of his fiancée.

"I LOVE MEETINGS WITH SUITS. I LIVE FOR MEETINGS WITH SUITS. I LOVE THEM BECAUSE I KNOW THEY HAD A REALLY BORING WEEK AND I WALK IN THERE WITH MY ORANGE VELVET LEGGINGS AND DROP POPCORN IN MY CLEAVAGE AND THEN FISH IT OUT AND EAT IT. I LIKE THAT."

The nudity scandal didn't seem to inter-
fere with the wedding plans, however. The
couple decided to hold the ceremony on
Madonna's birthday, August 16, and sent invita-
tions to the most important stars and starmak-
ers in Hollywood. They made elaborate plans
to hide the location of the wedding, an estate
perched on a cliff overlooking a private beach.
The guests were instructed to include a
phone number with their RSVP so they could be
called the day before the wedding and told
where to come.

Somehow, the location was discovered.
On the big day, press helicopters circled the
estate. (The fact that Sean Penn had written an

obsenity in large letters in the sand probably
helped them find the site.) Even the groom's
attempts to shoot down the helicopters didn't
deter the photographers. The wedding of the
year turned into a fiasco as the noise of the
helicopters drowned out the nuptial vows.

THE MARRIEDS AND THE MOVIES

After the wedding, the Penns began searching
for a project they could work on together. As it
happened, Madonna was approached by George
Harrison, former Beatle and now partner of
Hand Made Films, with a screwball comedy
called *Shanghai Surprise*, set in Hong Kong in
the thirties. Madonna would play a strait-laced

"I AM AFRAID THAT IN FIVE YEARS, ALL MY FRIENDS WILL BE DEAD."

"I ULTIMATELY END UP MAKING MY OWN WORK. I DON'T SIT AROUND WAITING FOR OTHER PEOPLE TO GIVE IT TO ME. I'VE HAD TO DO THIS TO ENSURE MYSELF CONSTANT EMPLOYMENT."

missionary who undergoes a sexual awakening. The role appealed to her, and there was an added bonus — Penn had the male lead, a sort of low-life Clark Gable. It was perfect. A project they could work on together, set in the exotic East. It would be more like a honeymoon than work.

Wrong! Their trailer was full of rats, and the local food made them sick. When they moved into a hotel in Hong Kong, Sean punched out a reporter who was following them. From there, things deteriorated to the point that the press dubbed the pair "the Poison Penns." Finally, after a stern lecture,

George Harrison and Madonna held a press conference to patch things up between the marrieds and the media.

But nothing could save the movie. It was a complete disaster. The critics pilloried it, and the audiences shunned it. Madonna quickly moved on to other projects that didn't involve her husband.

ON BROADWAY

Madonna's next project was also a flop. *Who's That Girl* was an utterly forgettable comedy co-starring a panther. Madonna's performance, like everything else in the film, was unconvincing.

But no matter. Madonna was on to other

things. She had read a new script, a play by David Mamet. Mamet was one of the best playwrights in the country, having written *American Buffalo*, *Sexual Perversity in Chicago*, and the Pulitzer Prize–winning *Glengarry Glen Ross*.

His new play, *Speed-the-Plow*, concerned two scheming Hollywood producers and an administrative assistant named Karen who tries to convince one of the producers to adapt a novel about nuclear war. Madonna loved Karen, whom she saw as "an angel of mercy who was coming down to save everybody."

Madonna took Mamet's play as seriously as she took her music. Unfortunately, her con-

cept of Karen was dramatically different from Mamet's and the director's. They wanted the audience to leave the theater wondering what kind of person Karen really was. During rehearsals, her lines were changed to make Karen more ruthless and conniving. Madonna, who was used to collaborating on all her projects, ended up feeling used and betrayed.

The worst heartbreak was that her efforts at serious acting had come to nothing. The audiences filled the theater as long as she played, but the reviews were almost unanimously unfavorable. One headline was simply, "No, She Can't Act."

GOODBYE PENN AND PEPSI

During the unsuccessful run of *Speed-the-Plow*, Madonna divorced Sean Penn. His jealous rages had become more and more dangerous. One story, unconfirmed but also undenied by Madonna, held that their final breakup occurred when Penn tied her to a chair in their Malibu house for nine hours. Now, free from a bad marriage and bad Broadway reviews, she moved on to her next project — a commercial for Pepsi-Cola.

This project promised to outdo all her previous ones. Her contract was for $5 million, and she was now in the ranks of previous Pepsi representatives, who included megastars

Michael J. Fox and Michael Jackson. What's more, the commercial was scheduled to air at the same time her new video, "Like a Prayer," premiered.

Unfortunately, the executives at Pepsi-Cola didn't bother to preview her video, which

mixed Catholic imagery with Madonna's usual sexual provocativeness, deeply offending many churchgoers. The only connection between the video and the commercial was their simultaneous air date, but that didn't matter to an angry public. Pepsi pulled the ad, hoping to run it

later, but a threatened boycott caused the company to drop the commercial altogether. While Pepsi was out a hot ad campaign plus the $5 million it had paid Madonna, the controversy only fueled Madonna's growing legend.

The album, *Like a Prayer*, was a popular and critical success. Perhaps more important, it was a personal victory. Working again with Steve Bray, Madonna had written songs that dealt with her personal demons — her relationship with Sean Penn, her family, and the church. It was as if she were saying goodbye to those things and moving on to something new. And she moved with a vengeance.

NEW HITS, NEW BOYFRIEND

Madonna's next coup contained equal measures of art, romance, and opportunism — a grand slam of three productions: her Blonde Ambition Tour, her provocative documentary *Truth or Dare*, and a leading role in the movie *Dick Tracy* — plus a romance with Hollywood's then-longest-running playboy, Warren Beatty.

Beatty had convinced Al Pacino, Dustin Hoffman, and James Caan to play comic villains in his movie about the comic-strip hero Dick Tracy. One part was uncast, that of nightclub singer and vamp Breathless Mahoney. When Madonna asked to read for the part, she was

mortified to learn that she wasn't even on the C-list let alone the A-list. Soon, however, she had an important advantage: She was dating the leading man.

Dick Tracy, for all its star power, did not join the super-grossing ranks of *Batman* and *Superman*. But it was quite a success for Madonna. Her reviews were good, and she worked a deal that allowed her to release her own album inspired by the film, *I'm Breathless.*

As the album hit the stores, Madonna launched the Blonde Ambition Tour, an extravaganza employing deco sets by her brother Christopher and outlandish outfits. The most shocking of the latter was a mannish suit with

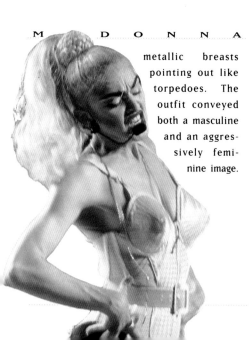

metallic breasts pointing out like torpedoes. The outfit conveyed both a masculine and an aggressively feminine image.

Madonna was not the only crossdresser in the show. Singing "Like a Virgin," she writhed on a red velvet bed, flanked by two figures with even larger and pointier breasts than her own.

This was the most ambitious project Madonna had ever attempted. And she decided it should be filmed. To direct the film, she chose Alek Keshishian. The twenty-six-year-old filmmaker had just completed a version of *Wuthering Heights* in which the actors lipsynched to famous singers' hits, including Madonna's.

Early on, Keshishian changed the nature of the project. He was originally supposed to film some backstage scenes to add interest to the onstage ones. But he found the backstage goings-on so fascinating that he sold Madonna on the idea of doing a documentary about the tour, rather than just filming the show itself.

THE DARING TRUTH

Madonna was undaunted by Keshishian's threats to film anything and everything on the tour. She allowed him to film her topless, seeing her doctor, waiting at home for Beatty to call, in bed with her entourage. After all, the film was called *Truth or Dare*.

Truth or Dare also showed some less sensational but nevertheless revealing

moments: Madonna micromanaging the tour; Madonna yelling at her manager about sound problems; Madonna spitting on the ground in front of the Toronto police when they threatened to close her down; Madonna pulling the cast together before a show to lead them in a prayer; Madonna waiting for her brother after a show; Madonna brushing off an old friend. The portrait is of a committed, creative artist, dedicated to her art but often more loyal to her career than to friends, lovers, or family.

The film was a sensation at the Cannes Film Festival. It was said that the second most difficult tickets to get at the festival were for

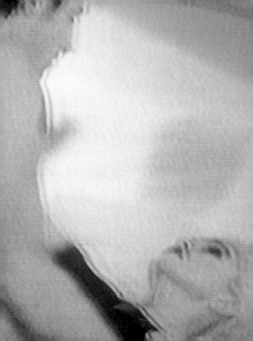

Truth or Dare. (The hardest ones to get were to the *Truth or Dare* party thrown by Madonna to celebrate the film's opening.)

It seemed that Madonna couldn't get any more revealing than this documentary. However, she kept coming up with new ways to shock the public. Her next video, "Justify My Love," was banned from MTV for its sexual content. Filmed in arty black and white, it depicted a variety of couples engaged in sexual encounters. While some of the couplings were homosexual (Madonna, for example, was shown being kissed by another woman) and one involved bondage, nothing explicit was shown. Nevertheless, the video was banned.

Madonna cried sexism: The sexual content of her video was no worse than that of other videos, and those made by male groups were allowed to air. MTV refused to change its decision. Ironically, the video's only airings were on network television programs reporting the controversy.

Instead of changing the video, Madonna released it in stores, thumbing her nose at MTV. Viewers willingly paid ten dollars a pop to see the video they couldn't see on MTV.

A League of Her Own

Shortly after *Truth or Dare*, Madonna played a minor part in *A League of Their Own*, a film

about the all-woman baseball league, then went right to work on *Body of Evidence*, which was panned. In between these two movies she produced *Sex*, a book of photographs and a loose diarylike narrative that was covered with plastic so it couldn't be read without buying. A controversy (what else?) ensued on talk shows and newscasts about whether the photos were art or pornography.

She also produced the album *Erotica* and a video of the title song based on *Sex*, which was played on MTV only after midnight. Later, less controvesial videos of two other songs from *Erotica* were released.

Madonna's singing career has soared.

"I WANTED TO BE A NUN.
I SAW NUNS AS SUPERSTARS."

"I KNOW I'M NOT THE BEST
SINGER. I KNOW I'M NOT
THE BEST DANCER. BUT I'M
NOT INTERESTED IN THAT.
I'M INTERESTED IN PUSHING
PEOPLE'S BUTTONS."

It appears that she will continue her acting career as well, but it remains to be seen if she can act the part of someone else. Most of her films have flopped. *A League of Their Own* succeeded in spite of, rather than because of, Madonna. Her only really good acting reviews came from *Desperately Seeking Susan* and *Dick Tracy*, in which Madonna basically played herself.

And perhaps that's the secret to her artistic success — playing herself. It is in that sense that she has been more successful as a singer performing her material. Through her songs, she has dared to express what most people keep private, as if she were sitting in a Catholic confessional.

Madonna readily admits that she isn't the best dancer or singer or even songwriter in the

world. But, while other rock stars play guitars, pianos, or synthesizers, Madonna's instrument is herself: *her* sound, *her* look, *her* life. And nobody plays it like she does.

I
JU
IMMACULA

VOLU

A CER

MADONN

SHAN
WH

The Basic

MADONNA

Visual

Library

V O L U M

JU

SHA

T

BOD

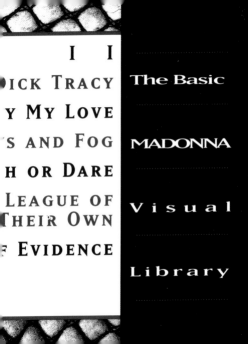

I I
ICK TRACY
Y MY LOVE
S AND FOG
H OR DARE
LEAGUE OF
THEIR OWN
EVIDENCE

The Basic

MADONNA

Visual

Library

TH

WH

BLO

The text of this book was set in Matrix, by
Snap-Haus Graphics, Dumont, New Jersey.

Design by
Diane Stevenson / SNAP-HAUS GRAPHICS